BUBBLE WRAP

THE BENEFITS BOOK

BY KEVIN MCFADDEN

Suite 300 - 990 Fort St
Victoria, BC, Canada, V8V 3K2
www.friesenpress.com

First Edition — 2016

ISBN
978-1-4602-7702-7 (Hardcover)
978-1-4602-7703-4 (Paperback)
978-1-4602-7704-1 (eBook)

1. Business & Economics, Insurance, Health

Distributed to the trade by The Ingram Book Company

TABLE OF CONTENTS

GRATITUDE

This book would not have been possible without the caring support of the many awesome people in my life. For years I pondered writing this book, but like countless other things it was "I should" instead of "I will". Robin Sharma, who I consider one of the world's premier leadership experts, inspired me at his astounding Titan Summit in Toronto, to thrust out of my comfort zone and push to my edges. It was at this Summit that I met my hero Richard Branson and made the decision to write this book and live my best life every day. I am eternally grateful to Robin for his message and encouragement to write this book. I am also very grateful to the wise souls Dr. James Rouse and Dennis Moseley Williams for following their life passion and mission of assisting people to be their very best. I draw strength and courage by following their inspiring messages regularly.

I have been blessed with having many mentors in my career. Jeff Aarssen gave me my start out of university in 1990 and hired me to join The London Life Insurance Company as an Employee Benefits Sales & Service Representative. Their world class training program allowed me to join an industry that I am very passionate about and provided me with the tools to hone my skills. Over my eight years with this incredible organization I was exposed to amazing people with whom I celebrated successes, shared failures and learned what true leadership is really about. I was privileged to work with very classy mentors such as John Koep and Gary Rusu who taught me at a young age the importance of family, community and doing the right thing every time.

I am grateful to George Sigurdson who facilitated my independent start in 1998 after my career with London Life. He assisted me to become an independent entrepreneur and follow my dreams and passion of creating remarkable value, building meaningful relationships and dutifully serving with humility.

Many of the people I worked with in the early years of my career are very close to me today. I am fortunate to regularly see many of them socially and through my involvement and ownership in the Benefits Alliance Group. John Goode, Ian Watson, Tony Fairfield and Paul Crossdale are dear friends and respected peers and I lean on them constantly for wisdom and support. They are some of the finest people I have ever known and I thank them for their encouragement as I journeyed to craft this book.

I have been so proud to work with my loyal and dedicated staff who over the years were nothing short of incredible. Debbie, Kim, Pam, Julie-Ann, Pam, Nancy, Krista, Carol and Christina all made an impactful difference, proudly serving our valued customer partners and supporting our vision. My loyal assistant Pam Kenyon is quite possibly the most bubbly and positive person on the planet, and her personality, loyalty and support is a gift. Daily she makes it possible for me to passionately serve and follow my dreams.

I am privileged to work with many talented specialists who help me stay focused and properly execute my business plans and strategy. Denise Zaporzan is an incomparable leadership consultant with a broad range of deep academic and industry experience. Denise has helped me at many pivotal stages of my business evolution and I also have her to thank for the incomparable Pam! My brilliant lawyer Grant Stefanson has guided me skillfully through transactions that were critical to my businesses progression. His leadership skills are especially admired when he captains our almost annual trip to Iceland to play in an international beer league hockey tournament. Doug Smith, my accountant is a numbers savant and has provided me with sage advice and council on all important financial matters that have required consideration. I have never met anyone who matches his trivia prowess, especially anything that is related to 1980's rock! The best part of these trusted advisors is that they are amazing people and I have the humbling fortuity of being their friend first and client second.

Without my family this book would have no meaning. My beautiful wife and life partner Colleen captured my heart in 1992 while I was on a boy's trip to the Calgary Stampede, and my life has never been the same. We still are in disagreement of who asked who to dance first at the "Golden Garter Saloon" and it is a debate I expect that will continue on into perpetuity. She is the most solid and amazing person I know who exudes grace and integrity and she inspires me every day. I make no important decision in my life without her council. We have dreamed together and built my proudest achievement – my family. My teenage daughters Alexa, Ashley and Roxanne are all incredible young women and my life's greatest gift. Harlee the Golden Retriever and Duke the Chocolate Lab require loving notable mentions too.

To help me frame the content of this book to meet the needs of my audience, I assembled a very talented steering committee of human resources and management professionals from across a variety of industries.

These leaders invested their time and were extremely generous with their deep wisdom and guidance. A heartfelt thank you to; Candice Foreman, Misty Fraser, Debbie Knott, Stacey McLeish, Linda Monforton, Richard Neill, Terry Otchenash, Joan Slater, Todd Trueman and Linda Young. Their trust and confidence in me means more than I can express.

My mom is the pillar of strength in our family and dad the quiet and wise patriarch. We lost my brother Trent to leukemia when he was ten and I was fifteen years old. It was my parent's solid marriage, dignity and love that allowed my sisters Laurie, Darcie and I to learn how to hold together as a family and deal with incredible loss. I am forever grateful to my parents for their love, support and guidance over my lifetime. I would not be the person I am today if not for them.

I had the unprecedented good fortune early in my career of being supported by an incredible and influential person. Debbie Pinder left a respected insurance company and a long stellar career to join me in 1999. If you have had the opportunity to watch the show Suits on Netflix you will know what I mean when I explain that Debbie was the character Donna. She was our client service guru, office manager, analyst and sometimes mother, performing every role tasked to her with skill and grace. Debbie was a driving force and an amazing worker who was smart, loyal and passionate about delivering the best experience to our customers every time. Whenever I would discuss my next far fledged idea, she would in her stoic way flash me a small smirk, sometimes roll her eyes, but would always execute the plan with precision.

The best way to describe Debbie's character and dedication is to a share a story about her. Early in the evolution of the company Debbie was uncharacteristically late for work one morning. I was sitting in my 19th floor office and heard sirens on the street below – little did I know it was an ambulance and Debbie was inside of it. A short while later I had a phone call from a bank employee who worked downstairs, explaining to me that Debbie had fallen outside on the street and broken her ankle very badly. I rushed over to the hospital and her ankle was indeed severely fractured. As always, she didn't complain but rather viewed her severe injury as a "small" inconvenience. Within days she had moved in with her mom and dad to care for her, and by her choice had set up a mobile command post with her leg in the air, laptop and phone close by and mom - the impromptu receptionist, greeting the many couriers growing familiar with our newest satellite office.

That was the kind of person she was. Debbie was a rare gem. Those of us who know her had the very good fortune of basking in the presence of a remarkable human being.

Sadly we lost Debbie in 2011 after a dignified and gracious battle with breast cancer. I would not be where I am in my career today without her.

I dedicate this book to her precious memory.

INTRODUCTION

WHY BUBBLE WRAP?

This book was written to assist employers who have or are considering implementing a meaningful employee benefits program for their valued employees. Employee benefits are designed to protect employees and their families from expected and unexpected life events and to make their lives easier, less stressful and more secure. With this "un-textbook," I hope to provide you with a useful reference to help you make good decisions as they relate to your company sponsored benefits program.

Bubble wrap to me is the perfect metaphor for employee benefits. It is easy to use, affordable and quite handy when protecting very valuable assets. Based on personal observations over twenty-five years of benefits advisory experience, the most successful companies I have worked with have a very common view of their employees. They view their people as their most valuable asset, avidly protect them and passionately treat them as if their future success and ultimate existence, as a company, unequivocally depends upon their people.

This then begs the question, *"how valuable do you view your employees and your company's ultimate success because of them"?* In addition, ask yourself if you believe your current benefits offering is designed to adequately bubble wrap your employees. If you are not sure ... that is ok, and I sincerely hope this book will help you to determine the answer to the question and better yet, offer options and solutions. By the way, I will be asking you other questions to ponder the answers, if you decide to read on. And please don't worry - there won't be a test at the end!

As an unrelated aside, I want to share a funny story with you. I don't know what it is, but there is something mysterious about bubble wrap. No matter what age a person is, it seems that an almost uncontrollable force exists that prevents one from succumbing to the innate desire to "pop". In a completely unscientific, accidental and impromptu study I stumbled into, I recently wore the bubble wrap blazer (that I am wearing on the cover of this book) to a well-attended Human Resources conference at which I was speaking. Following my session, curious about how people would react to me, I walked into the trade show section of the conference with the bubble garment still on.

Besides realizing how smoking hot it gets wearing a plastic suit jacket, two things happened. Firstly, everyone loved it and asked why the Hades I was wearing a bubble wrap blazer. Secondly, it seemed that the mass legion of HR trade show attendees wanted to pop my bubbles. It was really weird. Some were polite and asked permission but most couldn't control themselves and just had to do it. Pop, pop, pop. I had to leave or face the embarrassing reality of leaving a sweaty and tattered bubble wrapped mess - facing the difficult possibility of trying to convince our tailor to commission "version II." My wife Colleen experienced many a perplexed tailor who gave her weird looks when she asked if they could make us a custom tailored size forty-two bubble wrap blazer. She fortunately found said tailor with a good sense of humour and wonderful sense of adventure. I am happy to say that after many speaking engagements, bubble jacket "version I" still goes on tour with me and as a bonus, doubles as a comfy pillow when needed.

This book is purposely written in a fun manner that is easy to reference and read. It is not intended to read as a text book or a study of studies and is deliberately devoid of detailed statistics, boring charts, graphs, etc. My intention is to present to you an easy read with an abbreviated collection of observations, stories and good ideas and ok, some (hopefully interesting) stats. My esteemed Book Steering Committee told me to write it this way and I promised to listen to them. They also told me not to make it too long which was a relief, as I was planning on spending a distressing chunk of my summer preparing it. In the end it still took *way* longer to write than expected and ate up a big chuck of my summer (and fall and early winter). However I have no regrets and I am pleased with the end result. More importantly I hope you are too!

In my small way it is such a privilege to give back to an industry that has given me so much. I proudly share with you my handcrafted work that will hopefully provoke thought, encourage discovery, inspire discussion and ultimately drive positive change.

I sincerely hope you will enjoy reading Bubble Wrap and find it beneficial to you in your organizational leadership role.

With gratitude,

Kevin

CHAPTER 1

WHEN WE RAISE OUR CHILDREN

I debated whether or not to include this chapter, even before my editor advised me not to include it, as it has no relevance to "benefits" and the topics I wished to address in this book. I didn't disagree with the professional assessment but decided to include it anyway.

The enclosed words shared with me by Susan Rothery were some of the most profound I had read in a long time and they deeply resonated with me... so much so that I decided to open the book with them and leave the interpretation of relevance to you, the reader.

"When we raise our children, when we work with children, when we spend any amount of time with children, we are the best people we can be.

We encourage, we smile, we correct, we console, constantly aware that what we are doing is teaching them about this wonderful world and how it should be navigated.

They respond with bravery and laughter. We can see them thinking, assessing, judging, modeling how they should act based on what we teach them, connecting the dots and amazing us when they connect them in ways that delightfully surprise. It fills our hearts and makes us feel good, not only about ourselves but about them. They make us proud.

We don't think twice about being this generous. It is not an expectation. It is a fulfillment, a reason for being, a destiny.

We're reminded of all the important adults in our lives who guided us on our way – parents, grandparents, teachers, Brown Owls, Scout Leaders, religious leaders. We are in love with those memories. We remember how these people inspired us, how they made us feel, which was safe and important.

We remember what it felt like when we were the focus of such undivided attention. In return, we made them feel safe and important too because we were just kids and everything they did was awesome. We could trust them. Not always, but mostly because we also learned when to back off.

And yet somewhere along the way, between being on the receiving end of all this generosity as children and the giving end as adults, we installed conditions. It doesn't matter why – they got installed. We grew a thicker skin, we became more guarded, we learned not everyone can be trusted, and the result was that we forgot much of what we knew was right when it came to being guided and giving guidance, of teaching and being taught, of just mixing with the world at large. Bottom line: our generosity of spirit took a hit.

So?

If being generous, as we are with our children, can put a smile on our faces when our heads hit the pillow, then it's worth doing it a lot more. With everyone. The results will be exactly the same as they are with the little people in our lives. People we guide, mentor, manage, speak with, work with and play with will feel cared for, empowered, inspired, and we'll feel good about it, knowing that being selfless trumps the opposite every time. We've already learned when to back off, so no risk there. It's simply a matter of choice."

As a parent, family member, spouse, employer, friend, citizen, human being, think about these words and what they mean to you. For this brilliance, Susan I thank you.

Susan's eloquence came to me via DMW Strategic Consulting and the blog "Daily Transmission" that I receive daily and follow religiously. (http://moseleywilliams.com/blog/)

CHAPTER 2

ADVICE

One of the topics my Book Steering Committee seemed broadly interested in was how to select a benefits advisor and what to expect from them. Our industry seems to have a bit of an identify challenge by not mutually agreeing on what it is we should be consistently calling our profession. "We" are referred to commonly as benefits "brokers" or "consultants." However I prefer benefits "advisor" and will use this description when describing the role. Our job is actually quite easy to describe and we as benefits advisors provide information and layout options in a timely manner so that the employers we serve can make good informed decisions. Like all good vendor/supplier relationships, the foundation should be built on trust and confidence. As an employer your choices of a benefits advisor are divided into three distinct categories.

National consulting firms have head offices that are typically in larger urban centers with satellite offices spread out across regions. Most of these firms are larger publicly traded companies with international offices, while some are structured like a law firm with partners retaining a share of ownership. They generally work in the larger employer segment with defined benefit pension actuarial services included in their services platform.

Regional benefits advisors typically operate in a defined geographic area with one or more physical locations. The regional benefits advisor is typically an entrepreneurial owner-operated company with one or more shareholder/principals. Skilled regional advisors will have the ability to advise in multiple provinces. With the proper network they can also provide international benefits advice and counsel. Many of my peers, like myself, are fiercely independent and pride themselves on operating without the necessity of meeting scheduled shareholder financial expectations.

Insurance brokers/agents are also able to provide benefits advice and source product. While these practitioners are active in the marketplace as general practitioners, their specialty often leans toward life insurance and investment products. Many smaller employers are often well served by the insurance broker/agent in handling their benefits needs.

A good benefits advisor will have many years of experience with an excellent reputation for service, negotiation skills, relationships, and will always put their client's needs first. Our industry is professional and the large majority of my peers are skilled technically and do a good job of advising their clients properly. When I think of the "best of the best" of my industry peers, they have the following common traits: are tough on insurers but reasonable, obsessively deliver value, build communities, create amazing experiences, embrace change, amp technology, hire rock stars, communicate fluidly, learn passionately, charge fairly and have access to the entire marketplace of suppliers. It is a bonus if they are fun to deal with!

Your advisor is compensated for his or her work by commissions paid from the insurer or third party administrator, or on a fee for service basis. National consulting firms typically bill by the hour or project, however they also can be paid via commissions. Based on my experience most regional benefits advisors are paid a commission for their services using a retainer style of arrangement. It is difficult to confirm what a fair benefits advisory fee is, as each advisory situation is very different in terms of complexity, size of company, resources committed, special projects, reporting, etc. A commission amount under 5% of premiums for a medium to large employer and over 5% for small employers is a common investment for a qualified benefits advisor to assist you in the management of your program. I would recommend you have an open conversation with your benefits advisor about their compensation structure and the services that you require in return. A good benefits advisor will always provide full fee disclosure and deliver to the client with an excellent return on their advisory services investment. We are paid fairly for what we do and we need to consistently perform, adding value.

As advisors we are hired or appointed by a simple letter. It is referred to as an "agent of record" letter. It is a goofy name in my opinion and I would expect this terminology was coined in the venerable early days of our industry. Changing a benefits advisor is not complicated or arduous and if you are not feeling the love or seeing a ROI, I would encourage you have the "come to Jesus" chat (keep the Kleenex box nearby). If you feel it is time for a change, I would suggest you review the marketplace for reputable firms, create a short list of candidates and commence the interview process.

6 Tips for Selecting a New Benefits Advisor

1. *Who's in their "Tribe"?* Ask for references.

2. *Do they have Rock Stars?* Meet their people.

3. *Feel the love!* - Make sure you sense the "fit."

4. *Do they know what ASO stands for?* Make sure they are qualified to serve your needs.

5. *Do they understand the Experience Economy?* What are their "value adds"?

6. *Show me your best warrior pose!* Do they have a wellness advisory specialty?

CHAPTER 3

DRUGS INC.

By a Manitoba mile, the biggest healthcare benefit cost item for employers and employees is prescription drugs. We live in a society where modern medicine is universally accepted and big pharma has seemed to develop a prescription drug for almost every aliment. This chapter is not about the pros and cons of modern medicine and specifically prescription drugs, but rather important need-to-know facts for employers (and employees) about prescription drug options, costs, the pharmacies that sell and the manufacturers that produce. Countless articles and opinions have been published in the media and online. This chapter is written to help you, in layman's terms, wrap your head around the key topics and information.

Over my twenty-five years in the employee benefits industry, there has been one constant: the ever increasing cost of prescription drugs. This is why, when we talk about drug inflation, it is always a much higher number than the Consumer Price Index (CPI). Public demand, coupled with the financial incentives of manufacturers to research, develop, copy and market new drug offerings, has allowed society to have access to therapeutic treatments for everything from headaches and muscle pain to the treatment of chronic conditions such as arthritis, depression, hypertension and high cholesterol. Such myriad treatments - over the counter, oncology, prescription, brand name, generic, lifestyle, medical marijuana, biologic, etc. etc. - are all up for consideration for employers when they design their prescription drug plan for their employees. There are open formularies, managed treatments, mail order, wholesale, retail, provincially covered, not covered, drug cards, co-insurance, dispensing fee deductibles... The list of considerations goes on.

The one piece of advice I give to all my clients when it comes to prescription drug plans is this: *educate your employees on what they have and how to best shop for prescriptions*. With this, you will create a win-win. I will share with you a personal story that will relate to this advice.

Recently I had the not so good fortune of experiencing the crazy sensation of sciatica. I slipped a disk in my lower back while in the gym.

The disk pushed against my sciatic nerve, making my butt, thigh and lower leg down to my toes burn like I'd been stabbed by a white hot knitting needle. There are a few things that will bring a grown man to tears ... the ending of the movie Old Yeller, dropping and breaking a bottle of twenty year old scotch, and sciatic nerve pain. I hobbled down to the sports injury clinic, saw a doctor and he offered "nothing we can do but let it go away on its own – but I will prescribe you 28 - 500mg tablets of Naproxen (the over the counter name is Aleve). Take two a day and see me in two weeks".

I decided to practice what I preach to my clients and drove straight from the clinic (one butt cheek on the car seat the other raised – sciatic nerve suffers will relate) to Costco to have my prescription filled. My prescription was filled in fifteen minutes, I handed over $9.22 and was on my way. Well not really, I also bought a beef tenderloin for $89 and a six-pack of underwear for $19. As a result, the prescription turned out to be very expensive when I averaged in the cost of the tenderloin and super-sized pack of gitch.

Note to reader - if you can demonstrate purchasing restraint at Costco you will be rewarded with the lowest priced prescriptions in the marketplace. Buy the way, I will share with you a little secret ... you don't need a Costco membership to access their pharmacy.

I often wondered what that $9.22 prescription would have cost had I filled it at another full service retail pharmacy. I was sharing my story one day with a new client who was interested in discussing containing their prescription drug claims/costs, when a bright light when off.

I returned to the office and asked our team to do a quick research project to survey local pharmacies on their price of filling the exact 28 x 500mg Naproxen prescription. My intrepid team put on their Columbo hats and went to work. Their findings were dramatic. Of the eight other pharmacies surveyed, the next closest price to fill the Naproxen prescription was $15.00 and the highest was $21.00 with the average price being $17.93. So think about this: if one single prescription can cost 228% more from one pharmacy to another, what would be the effect if all your employees filled their prescriptions at the place that cost $21 versus $9.22? If I told you which pharmacy charged $21 for the Naproxen prescription you would instantly recognize the name.

Now in fairness to the pharmacies that provide excellent value added service and convenience, the big box solution may not meet everyone's needs. In fact, many consumers have an excellent relationship with their pharmacist and the service and advice they provide can be very valuable.

It is important, however, that you educate your employees on the pricing differences between pharmacy chains. If your benefits advisor hasn't already provided you with it, ask for the *dispensing fee cost survey by pharmacy chain* and share it with your employees. Unless you have a plan that pays 100% of the cost of the prescription, your employees will be interested in how they can save money too.

If you don't have a prescription drug card plan, it is time to consider it. A benefits plan without the drug card worked well in the 80's even the 90's. The long held assumption and objection towards the introduction of the drug card was that it would add additional costs to the program. The phenomenon is commonly referred to in the industry as the "shoebox effect," meaning some members lose or forget to submit their claims to the plan, hence claims and ultimately costs are lower. While there is some validity and logic to this, it is an antiquated old school belief. A drug card creates point of purchase convenience because the member is not out of pocket any money unless there is a co-insurance or dispensing fee deductible. With online claims submission, the vast majority of the shoebox effect has been reduced or eliminated. The shoebox effect will be offset over the longer term as the plan sponsor gains control of their drug management. Your proactive benefits advisor can slice and dice data for illustration. In addition, plan option modelling can be done easily and pharmacies will only charge what the electronic system limit will allow. Most importantly your employees will value the plan more as they will not be out of pocket or have to submit claims manually. They will love the new found convenience.

I like two specific prescription drug plan designs because they are clean, easy to understand and introduce a degree of cost sharing with the employees, if that is an objective. Both include **generic substitution** which helps control ingredient costs, by limiting coverage of brand name drugs to the lowest cost equivalent.

All claims for drugs with a generic version are cut back to the lowest cost equivalent. The first plan design is an 80% co-insurance plan whereby the employee pays 20% of each claim at the point of sale.

If the employees are educated on the pricing differences by pharmacy chain (remember the Costco example) then they know that their choice as a consumer will impact both their personal costs and the costs of the overall plan.

The second plan design is a 100% coverage option with the dispensing fee deductible paid for by the employee at the point of sale. Similar to the first plan design illustrated, if the employees are educated (remember to ask your benefits advisor for a dispensing fee survey by pharmacy), they will know that their out of pocket cost per prescription for the dispensing fee will range from $5 to $15 depending on where they chose to shop. If your objective is to provide a fair, easy to understand plan with some sharing of costs, then either of the above plans should work well for you.

All drug plans have a formulary which is simply the list of drugs that are covered under the plan. Plan sponsors have a typical choice of formularies that are described as "managed" or "open". The most common and least restrictive is the **open formulary**. The distinction depends on which drugs are covered or not and any associate restrictions or limitations.

Managed formularies typically are set and managed by a tall foreheads committee of clinicians and practitioners. This may include physicians and pharmacists, and other health and or industry professionals. The committee bases its decisions on clinical evidence from literature or reference materials, from expert opinions, and cost/benefit studies. Information may also be obtained from peer-reviewed journals and pharmaceutical companies.

The committee assesses each drug based on its clinical merits, its relative cost-effectiveness and its place in therapy, versus other comparable treatment options. It then makes decisions to list the drug, not list it or list it with limitations or criteria.

I have witnessed both formularies working well in real life applications. The key consideration in introducing a managed formulary is to understand the potential cost savings that may be generated and also understanding what the potential downside may be. The downside is the percentage of employees who will be impacted *and* if the savings offset any negative perception, which the employees might have, of the limitations of the plan. I have seen some conversions to a managed formulary not go so well. Angry employees, HR resources tied up answering claim questions and low employee satisfaction, as seen on survey scores, can be the by-product.

Proper communication to employees and a degree of flexibility when required, are paramount to the successful install of a managed formulary. A fulsome discussion with your benefits advisor is recommended before you tinker with an open formulary.

Biologics are newer to the marketplace. They are generally very expensive medications made from living organisms to treat conditions such as psoriasis and rheumatoid arthritis. Biologic drugs work by targeting the harmful attacks from the immune system that cause symptoms. Some brand name biologic drugs include: Amevive, Enbrel, Humira, and Remicade. Health case management and assertive claims adjudication help ensure that lower cost options are considered and if they are appropriate for the plan member's condition. Management and adjudication confirm if the treatment is delivering appropriate health outcomes. This overseeing also ensures that if biologics are prescribed, a cost benefit analysis is done to safeguard clinical appropriateness, as well as protect the plan against potential additional claims charges which could mount into tens of thousands of dollars. There are insurers and third party administrators who have this extra layer of claims adjudication and diligence.

This type of diligence will determine the value of new drugs coming to market, based in part on the publicly available information from the Canadian Agency for Drugs and Technologies in Health. This resource reviews drugs and makes reimbursement recommendations to Canada's federal, provincial and territorial public drug plans to guide their drug funding decisions. The goal is to ensure the patient receives proper therapeutic application and that the plan sponsors' costs are aligned most efficiently with appropriate treatment options. The intent of the process is to ensure that the best outcome for the best value is achieved.

If I can summarize this chapter with some clear advice it would be this:

Spend time with your benefits advisor on the topic of prescription drug coverage. Get an understanding of how much your company is spending every year on prescription drugs, what inflation levels you are experiencing and if biologic drugs are being claimed. Ask for reporting that breaks down the types of drugs being claimed by therapeutic class and from which pharmacies your employees are purchasing their prescriptions. Review plan design options such as co-insurance, formulary changes and dispensing fee deductibles.

Investing time and energy into this review will be a valuable exercise for your company and its employees.

CHAPTER 4

FLEX APPEAL

Flex is sexy and the law of attraction and retention is king in the competitive employment jungle.

Studies and surveys have confirmed over many years that employees want flexibility in their benefit plans. In fact, 91% of respondents to a recent employee benefits survey (SCHS) agreed they would like to be able to choose specific benefits that are best suited for their personal situation.

"Our benefits suck". This is a harsh statement but one that many employers have heard from some employees. Maybe the benefits plan lacks variety or pizzazz. If your benefits plan was an action figure it could be a Ken Doll - plain, boring

and uptight. For the record, it is widely speculated that Barbie and Ken were only friends and she had other love interests despite his claim to be her boyfriend, but that's another matter.

Flexible benefit plans come in a variety of options such as: modular, cafeteria or health care spending accounts (HCSA). All flexible i.e. "flex" benefit options serve a purpose and have associated likes and dislikes by both employees and employers. There is no right answer, however three options employers can consider to add flexibility to their benefits plans are as follows:

Modular flex plans offer employees a choice from a number of prepackaged plan options. Think Bob Barker and Showcase #1, #2, & #3. The better the Showcase the more the employee will be asked to dip into his or her pocket and pony up. These types of plans are generally well received but need to be logically designed and employers should offer no more than *three options* from which to choose. I recommend an employer have at least two hundred employees before considering this option.

Cafeteria flex plans are very descriptive of this option and the name "cafeteria" is well suited.

The employees browse the enticing choices, fill their tray and then check out at the register. If you have eaten at IKEA you get the picture... "hmmm let me see... Marinated Salmon Wrap, Haddock and Chips, oh God YES the Swedish Meatballs!!"

These plans are great for employees, however they are more challenging to administer, more expensive to provide (unlike the meatballs), and require a very high level of communication to employees. I recommend a company has at least one thousand employees before considering this option. Size definitely matters here.

A Health Care Spending Account flex option (my favorite) is a pre-determined amount of money provided to employees at the beginning of each benefit year for reimbursement of their medical and dental expenses - similar to their own personal benefits bank account. Think bank account that can only be spent on boring and responsible items, (fashionable eyeglasses and relaxation massages aside). Canada Revenue Agency has a long list of approved items that employees can spend money on using their HSCA dollars such as regular dental work, medical marijuana (heavy on the medical), gluten-free products, laser eye surgery and cancer treatment in or outside of Canada. One particular insurance carrier has a product in the form of a VISA card loaded up with employer flex dollars. Any size of company can add a HSCA to its benefits plan and it can be very affordable.

Some companies have taken the health care spending account to another level and offer **expanded reimbursement items**. Allowances for purchases of parking, public transportation, Fit Bits, iPhone wellness apps, yoga classes, gym memberships, sports equipment, bikes, treadmills, etc. have been added. Keep in mind that these items are not typical CRA HSA approved eligible expenses and would create a taxable benefit scenario for the employee. However, imagine the positive impression this type of program would generate on your employees.

I will let you in on a little secret. If you offer your employees an annual spending account, on average, only 75% of the dollars offered are generally spent in total. For example ... if your company offers an annual $400 spending account allowance, the average employee will only use $300. Here's the good part - you get the credit for offering $400 and it costs you only $300. ***Shhhh!***

In summary, as an employer you need to ask yourself if your employee benefits program is a Ken Doll? With some energy and effort it could be a Flex Armstrong. If I have lost you, Google this obscure toy that was popular in the 70's and you will get my point.

Ever wonder if the rumours about Barbie and GI Joe were true? ☺

CHAPTER 5

PAY ME NOW OR PAY ME LATER

How you pay for your benefits plan can often mean the difference in thousands of dollars annually as well as potentially significant long term savings.

Before we go there, let's draw some comparisons. This may be a mind shift for you, but think of your insurer in the way a casino operates. The casino requires a large volume of new and repeat customers, accepts risk as a component of its business model and is a publicly traded company with quarterly and annual profitability requirements. In simple terms it needs to take in more than it pays out. It may lose, it may win, but overall if it is profitable, it wins. What I mean by that is it takes in premium, pays claims, covers the expenses and is typically left with a surplus/ profit. If not, the shareholders get grumpy. Sometimes the profit is large and sometimes it is smaller but the entire business model is based on winning more than losing. The "casino mathematicians" are the actuaries who are highly educated business professionals, analyzing the financial consequences of risk and pricing.

Insurers provide a very valuable service to individuals and employers; our industry would not exist without them. They have created valuable products and services, accepting large risk that many of their customers cannot absorb.

If you have been to Las Vegas, or any casino for that matter you will know that coming out a winner happens less than more. That is the simple premise of why casinos exist and are profitable.

The same holds true for insurers who charge premiums and accept risk by paying claims that may exceed the premium collected. I believe that plan sponsors can take on some risk and reduce the house edge that inherently exists for insurers who collect health, dental and short term disability premium and pay out claims. My point of all this comparison of odds, winning and losing, is to point out an important consideration of how to pay for your health, dental and short term disability programs.

If you are prepared to take on some measured risk but continue to protect against the calamitous claims, your rewards can be measurable and meaningful. I think I am going to hear from some of my insurer partners about this casino analogy ☺.

There are essentially two types of benefits funding contracts that exist; fully insured and ASO or Administrative Services Only.

A fully insured contract is a common way for employers to fund their health, dental and short term disability plans. Fully-insured funding arrangements offer predictable monthly premiums, guaranteed protection for all covered claims and simplicity. With a fully-insured plan, a company pays a fixed monthly premium to the insurance company, regardless of the plan's claim costs. It is the insurance company that assumes the financial and legal risk of loss if claims exceed projections. It works very well if your claims exceed your targeted amount... that is until your annual renewal ... where you can guess what happens next.

Administrative Services Only: For the right situation I am a very strong proponent of ASO arrangements. Under an ASO contact, the plan sponsor/employer funds its own employee benefit plan for such expenses as medical, dental and short term disability claims. They engage an outside firm such as an insurer or third party administrator to perform specific administrative services such as adjudicating and paying the claims for a fee usually paid as a percentage of the claims value.

Many of our clients with an ASO contract use what I call the “Bucket Method”. The employer sets up a stand-alone bank account (the bucket), and deposits their premiums into it. The insurer or TPA, with permission of course, accesses the account and pays the employee’s claims out of the bucket. If more money is placed in the bucket than is needed to pay claims and administrative expenses, then there is a surplus, which is the employer’s. This is simple and effective - and often a happy dance breaks out at renewal time.

Any pooled benefits (Life Insurance, Dependent Life Insurance, Accidental Death & Dismemberment coverage, Long Term Disability, and Critical Illness) remain with an insurance company and it carries the full risk of a large claim.

An employer also needs to consider two other stand-alone forms of insurance coverage under an ASO arrangement:

1. **Out Of Country Insurance** provides emergency medical coverage for employees when traveling outside Canada.

2. **Stop Loss Insurance** is provided when the employer indicates how much Stop Loss Insurance coverage they want (e.g. $10,000 per employee per year, etc.). In the event that one of the employees was prescribed an expensive drug such as a biologic, the company's deposited premium dollars would have to pay for the employee's claim up to the Stop Loss amount. Any amount over the Stop Loss amount would be insured. Think of it as an annual dollars ceiling.

Historically the advantages of administrative services only (ASO) plans had been accessible only to larger employers. Smaller employers had fewer options in group benefits plan design and funding. Increasingly, employers sought cost control and flexibility and the market responded by opening up ASO options to smaller companies. Today a company with as few as 25 employees can consider an ASO option for funding part of its benefits.

Employers may be concerned that ASO funding is unpredictable, as month-to-month claims can fluctuate. It can be challenging for smaller employers in particular to fund $2,000 in claims one month and $6,000 the next, for example. Budgeted ASO plans can offer relief from this concern.

A predictable fixed premium each month based on the group's historical claims patterns can be set up with a budgeted ASO plan. This would be a similar situation to a monthly fixed estimated utility bill that is adjusted after a specific duration.

Monthly financial reporting of surpluses or deficits provides assurance that the company doesn't receive a renewal "surprise". If claims exceed the budgeted paid premium amount, the employer is responsible for the deficit. If claims are less than the premium, the surplus belongs to the employer.

It is important that your benefits advisor, in concert with the TPA or insurer, keep you abreast of the ongoing financial situation with monthly reporting, so that you may monitor closely and avoid the "surprise".

So, why consider an ASO contract? Many companies, fed up with seemingly automatic annual increases in their employee benefits premiums, have found that by self-insuring some benefits via an ASO plan, they are able to keep their benefits costs down over a long period of time, often many years.

Our clients who utilize ASO contracts are believers. Talk to your benefits advisor about the ASO option and have him or her prepare an analysis of the pros, cons and historical surpluses you may have enjoyed had you been on an ASO contract. Changing to ASO could be the best financial decision you ever make regarding your benefits program. If you are already drinking the Kool Aid, cheers to you!

CHAPTER 6

COOL BENEFITS

Free coffee, an RRSP match and casual Fridays aren't always enough to cut it these days. Employers are getting more creative and investing to make sure they attract and retain top talent. The employee benefits they're offering range from simply fun to over-the-top "you are a rock star" treatment.

Employers are continually looking at new ways of providing an interesting array of benefits, expanding the traditional definition beyond regular health and dental plans. Some employers now refer to the benefit offering as their 'Suite of Benefits and Services' rather than simply a group insurance or retirement plan. This trend has been brought on by the shortage of available talented and qualified employees in today's competitive job marketplace, which can be best described as 'free agency.' It has also been spurred on by the newer generation of employees with their unique and arguably sensible view of the world and employment options.

In an effort to attract and retain their prized talent, employers are helping employees in a range of offerings: to save for their children's education, to learn how to eat, sleep and exercise better, to finance the purchase of healthy lifestyle goods and services, to find the lowest mortgage rates or even to insure their cat or dog. There is a push to "out create" the competition with respect to treating employees like rock stars. Positive impacts on recruiting, engaging and retaining employees are being measured while boards of directors are taking notice of the results.

It was not long ago that it would be a stretch to use word "cool" and benefits in the same sentence. That now appears to be changing. While the platinum standard in the rock star benefit category seems to be held by companies like Google in the Silicon Valley, Canadians are still pretty cool and many of our companies are punching above their weight class in coolness. Some recent recipient companies for the "Canada's Top 100 Employers" and "Canada's 50 Best Employers" award and some of the cool benefits they offer are described below.

Accenture Inc. runs a leadership development program for women, in which senior-level female employees are matched with a mentor for one-on-one coaching.

Birchwood Automotive Group offers employees on his or her 90th day at Birchwood lunches with a senior executive to discuss their experience at the automotive group. Workers earn "Birchwood Bucks" by hitting financial targets and can use them at a live auction to bid on prizes such as an Xbox and other gaming systems, as well as travel vouchers and cash.

Bombardier Aerospace provides unionized employees with DB plans, and gives newly hired non-unionized employees the choice between a combination DB and DC plan, or a fully DC plan.

Canadian Security Intelligence Service encourages employees to stay fit with an onsite fitness facility, instructor-led yoga, pilates, cardio classes and nutrition workshops.

Ceridian Canada Ltd. offers an animal insurance subsidy plan that covers up to 80% of veterinary costs.

EllisDon Corporation has an unlimited policy for time off. Employees are permitted requests for days off as they need them, rather than according to a vacation schedule.

L'Oréal Canada Inc. offers subsidies for professional accreditation, online courses and international training in Paris and New York. *(ah, excuse me, you missed Winnipeg?!)*

MNP LLP offers its Balance Subsidy program to reimburse the costs of activities that promote physical, mental or emotional wellness, including gym memberships, music classes and programs that help workers lose weight or quit smoking.

Manitoba Hydro has a centrally-located head office featuring roof top terraces, a six storey glass atrium and a twenty-four metre waterfall that moderates air humidity. New employees start accruing three weeks of paid vacation allowance, working toward a maximum of seven weeks paid vacation in addition to personal paid days off.

Molson Coors Canada runs a Molson Beer Academy—an in-house training program that includes courses on brewing techniques, beer tasting and brand awareness. *(I like this one!)*

PricewaterhouseCoopers LLP encourages employees to take time off during slow periods so they can properly prepare for the next rush season.

Royal Bank of Canada rewards staff by offering a week-long cruise to the seven hundred top-performing employees.

SaskTel provides an academic scholarship program, of up to $3,000 per child, for employees' children who pursue post-secondary education.

Telus Corporation offers an annual $500 "life balance account" that employees can use for anything they feel helps maintain their personal health. *(See Chapter 4 Flex Appeal).*

WestJet Airlines Ltd. features an employee share purchase plan that lets employees receive up to 20% of their gross regular earnings in WestJet shares with a 100% company match.

Another cool benefit that is offered in the marketplace is a Group RESP and TFSA. These programs work similar to a Group RRSP and they allow employees the opportunity to save for their children's education or create tax free growth on non-registered savings. Payroll deductions make it easier for the average employee to save money for something they feel strongly about but don't necessarily have the discipline to plan and save for.

With more than half of all households in Canada having pets, vet bills are a regular expense for many families. Vet bills can often be thousands of dollars and these unexpected costs may mean that pets are not treated adequately because the owners cannot afford the treatment, or a family's monthly budget is sent sideways. With affordable premiums and much interest from pet owning employees, employers such as Ceridian have allowed employees access to this new benefit at work. Petplan has partnered with benefits advisors who are helping companies set up Pet Insurance for their employees. Insuring a Rover can now take on a new and very different meaning!

My first tattoo was a yin-yang symbol. Ok I admit, in the spirit of full disclosure, it was a temporary henna, applied by my daughter Alexa.

I know what you are thinking,"wuse" *(Urban Dictionary definition... a weak, cowardly, or ineffectual person who works in or closely with an accounting department)*. My apologies to the accountants reading this and by the way, I am jealous, as I aspired to be an accountant in my first year of university until I received my marks back ...Introduction to Accounting: "D". Ouch! Hmmm, *Marketing* ... that major looks sweet.

Chinese philosophy, the yin-yang, describes how apparently opposite or contrary forces are actually complementary, interconnected, and interdependent in the natural world, and how they give rise to each other as they interrelate to one another. Yin and yang can be thought of as complementary forces that interact to form a dynamic system in which the whole is greater than the assembled parts. Businesses that really want to make an impact with their employee benefits understand this ancient concept as one of the most effective ways to make a difference for workers. Many businesses offer benefits that allow for better work-life balance. My friend Dr. James actually refers to it as a work life "blend" which to me has great meaning based on today's reality. Improvements of family leave benefits are occurring that assist new parents and individuals who are helping to take care of elderly parents. Telecommuting and flexible scheduling options that enable staff members to attend their child's soccer game and still meet work responsibilities, are expanding. Other work-life "blend" benefits that are becoming more common include everything, from nap rooms to nursing rooms for new mothers, to on-site child care, to EAP's that help employees better manage the cards that life dealt them. (See Chapter 12 Wellness)

Corporate sponsored wellness is gaining huge momentum in Canada. Companies are starting to connect the dots between wellness, productivity, talent acquisition and ultimately profitability. There are a multitude of options and the creative opportunities for employers are infinite. I believe this is the new frontier of corporate sponsored benefits and the early adopters will be rewarded. (See Chapter 12 Wellness).

So how does your benefits program stack up? Is it a *Moped? Harley? Chevette? Corvette?*

Pee Wee? or *P. Diddy?* If your benefits program is getting sand kicked in its face, then perhaps it is time to bulk up with some of the new and innovative *"Jack LaLanne"* benefits available to employers, many at little or no cost.

CHAPTER 7

BENEFITS COMMUNICATION

“Benefits are only as good as they are understood”.

I have been saying this to my clients for years. It is a simple statement but one that I believe captures the critical importance of a robust benefits communication campaign.

Benefits are where the needs of employees and their families and the needs of a business intersect. Benefits can account for almost 20% of total compensation spending, if government benefits are included. An effective communication program helps your company make the most of its investment. Effective communication also helps you find and retain top talent, keep them (and their families) healthy and productive, reduce overall health care costs and even improve your company's financial performance.

Getting people to pay attention to their benefits starts with making information accessible.

A very good way to do this is by putting benefits information on a stand-alone company branded website if possible, outside the corporate firewall. Many companies will also include benefits information on the company intranet site. When you put your benefits online, you give employees and families a single destination to act on their benefits or find answers to questions - anywhere, anytime.

For your employees, your benefits website will help them find the information they need fast - minimizing frustration, enhancing user experience and inspiring trust. It will also help them see their benefits holistically, rather than as a patchwork of providers and administrators. Paper booklets are still very common however, they get lost, outdated or you may have more than one booklet, based on how many suppliers you have.

For you, a benefits website provides a platform for ongoing communications. Even better, it may save you thousands in printing or mailing costs.

A benefits website lives on, long after dense enrollment guides and booklets are forgotten or get thrown away. Getting online is the most important investment you can make in your benefits communication.

Where to start?

Do some soul-searching, then develop your strategy. A communication strategy ties together your goals and communication channels - including your benefits website. Know your company. What drives your business results? How do your benefits attract the right people? How do they keep people engaged and focused at work? How will your efforts be measured?

- **Know your employees**.

  Who are they? What kind of families do they have? What motivates them? What keeps them up at night? How do those answers change, based on job category? What about other demographics?

- **Dive deeply into your benefits**.

  What does total compensation look like today, and how do you expect it to change in the next three years to respond to business needs? What behaviors do you want to change? Don't forget about the administrative piece. Where do your employees get stuck? Where are the messy areas of the company's experience? Find them and remove the pain points.

- **Build a feedback loop.**

  Listen to your employees and their families by creating feedback channels, surveying them, (surveymonkey.com is great) and conducting focus groups. Start with simple approaches like email surveys or focus groups - both of which are very effective. You want to learn about how your employees think and feel, what they know and what they want. Armed with this information, you can develop persuasive, effective communications that achieve the intended results.

- **KEEP TALKING**

  In the past, employees heard from you about once a year, when it was time to enroll or renew and you told them what their increases were. There was a time when that was sufficient, but now, employees are shouldering more of the financial risk for today's health expenses and tomorrow's financial security. They have to make choices on flex plans and retirement programs (Pension, DPSP, RRSP). They need to take a more active role in their health and finances to understand their plans and participate all year long. Support employees by giving them tips, reminders and updates throughout the year using every communication vehicle possible. Focus on pain points and missed opportunities, like HSA deadlines, year-end benefit limits and simple ways to take advantage of benefits. Offer smart ideas exist like upping employee RRSP contributions when bonuses are announced.

- **Give your employees context**.

  Share the background on your benefits package. Connect business issues with specific benefits. Be relevant. If the nightly news is talking provincial health care, or government pension plans, don't be afraid to give the company's point of view or acknowledge that you don't have all the answers. If changes are coming, tell employees exactly what changes you're making to their benefits plan, and why. That way, year-to-year changes won't be so alarming. When you communicate this way, employees will trust and depend on you in good times; then they're much more likely to listen during times of uncertainty. Your benefits website can tie into the broader communication efforts, building trust and a two-way dialogue on all business issues.

- **Embrace social media — it's here to stay.**

  Too many people still think of social media as a way to waste time, share pictures and play games. But social media tools give us easy, low-cost and effective ways to communicate throughout the year. They are perfectly suited for benefits. New platforms are available through smart phones. Many of your employees are accustomed to using social media to get the information they need; there's no reason you shouldn't take advantage of these tools for benefits, too.

  Getting started doesn't have to be overwhelming. Focus on these:

- **Starting small.**

  Incorporating a blog into your benefits website is the easiest way to get started with social media - and one of the least expensive ways to keep your website fresh.

- **Setting a realistic schedule.**

  Posting a few times a month is plenty. Update your communications calendar so you know what's going out when.

- **Keeping dialogue open.**

  Let employees comment on a blog, send questions via Twitter or attend virtual meetings. Then answer their questions and concerns. Keeping the door open is the best way to earn respect and loyalty from your employees. You can even set up your blog so that it's moderated —meaning no comments are posted until you review them.

  Talk to your people like people.

  "The company needs to control costs." "The company must make changes." "The company provides a health care plan."

  Phrases like that don't connect to real people's lives. Benefits are really about employees and their families. Remember they aren't benefits experts. You'll communicate most effectively when you think about their needs and talk to them like real people without jargon and legalese.

Ask yourself what's meaningful to employees and their families. The magic in benefits communication happens when what's good for your employees is also good for your company. Create a strategy that puts your employees first and articulates your goals in plain language. Your employees will see what's in it for them, and you'll get better outcomes.

Make it easy for employees to take action.

Benefits used are benefits valued. The best way to help employees appreciate programs is to encourage their use. You already have the information you need to do this. The next step is to take that information and organize it in a purposeful and strategic plan that guides your ongoing communications efforts.

- **Have a call to action**.

  Focus on action-oriented communications. Creating a sense of urgency will help overcome inertia especially if you offer a retirement matching program that not all employees take advantage of. "Free Money - *Hello*"

- **Make it relevant**.

  Give your employees targeted information, tips and examples based on their age and family situation.

- **Do the math**.

  Be specific about what will affect costs and how new changes in costs compare to current choices. Show real numbers and don't shy away from details that help with understanding. If you are asking the employees to pay for the LTD benefit explain why.

- **Take it step by step**.

  Be clear about steps to enroll or how to use the insurer tools, so employees don't get frustrated with a cumbersome administrative system or process.

- **WORK SMART**

  You don't have to do it alone! There are countless tools and resources out there that you can use for free to help you meet your goals. You can also promote free services to your employees that support your benefits strategy.

Your insurer or administrator and other program providers should be delivering top quality communication materials that you can incorporate into your own efforts.

Always have high expectations of how your benefits advisor and other vendors support your communications effort. Your benefits advisor is likely not a communications specialist, however he or she should be called upon to source relevant material for communication, or to source a design and marketing company to build a communications platform, if you decide to invest in external resources.

- **Beg, borrow and leverage.**

  Look for existing resources, tool kits, tip sheets and more, to coordinate and personalize. Look no further than your advisor or the web.

  Benefits Canada and Benefits and Pension Monitor are two Canadian publications that feature content exclusively focused on benefits and are great resources that exist to make your life easier, offering best practices, expert opinion, content and countless other resources. Both publications have a website with hundreds of archived papers and articles (even some of mine!). Don't be afraid to ask your benefits advisor to chime in on anything related to benefits. That is our job and that is what we are paid to do.

- **Find ways to get face-to-face.**

  Almost everyone would love to have you sit down with them, one-on-one, and explain your benefits and tell them what to do. That's not always practical in many medium to large organizations, but you don't have to lose a personal touch altogether. If you can get your people together in a room town hall style, nothing beats it. Have your advisor speak to the plan as an independent third party speaking from experience. We will have a better impact in promoting the merits of the plan and their appreciation of it - it's our job.

Simulate the sentiment of a one-on-one conversation by using:

- **Video conferences and webinars**.

  These can be a nice substitute for in-person meetings. Consider doing a series throughout the year or targeting the needs of different employee groups. You can also use that format for Q&A sessions. We regularly host video conferences and webinars for our clients who have employees in different geographic areas of the country. Roadshows are more of an investment, but we do these often to ensure the personal touch which aims at critical benefits messaging to be clearly delivered. This is common when a new benefit is added such as a retirement program or when we are assisting the merging of two companies.

- **Managers**.

  Empowering your managers connects them to the company more closely and helps keep employees engaged, too. Give managers a communications preview - before distributing to employees - and request their in-person engagement.

  You may not want managers trying to answer benefits questions, but they should always know where to direct employees and also understand the context for changes. Ask your benefits advisor to do a training session for your managers.

- **Measure your results**.

  After all of your hard work launching that big program, it is easy to let measurements fall by the wayside, but don't take your eye off the ball. Various data sources like the ones outlined below can help you measure your progress and give you a big-picture view of what's working and what can be better. Use that insight to fine-tune your communications, refine your approach and get closer to your goals.

- Meeting attendance tracked
- Surveys (as mentioned I like Survey Monkey)
- Focus groups (ask your employees for valuable feedback on their benefits)
- EAP utilization reports
- Wellness participation and tracking
- Retirement plan enrollment

- Claims data (disability, health, dental)
- HSA balances

Feeling inspired? Awesome! Overwhelmed? Talk to your advisor. Armed with inspiration and information, you're one step closer to breakthrough results with your benefits communication*.

**This insightful chapter was made possible by the brilliant content extensively referenced from the Benz Communications White Paper "Creating Results With Benefits Communications" authored by Jennifer Benz. A special thank you to Jen and Benz Communications for their insightful work and generosity of their intellectual property. https://www.benzcommunications.com/sites/default/files/Creating%20results%202014_0.pdf*

Benz Communications is based in San Francisco and is a leading North American communication firm specializing in employee benefits. www.benzcommunciations.com

CHAPTER 8

TIPS, TRICKS AND THOUGHTS

This chapter is a mixed bag of thoughts, observations, ideas and opinion. The intent is that you may glean some nuggets from this miscellaneous chapter to apply at your workplace.

In no particular order here goes:

A European study found that people who drank a 12-ounce sugar-sweetened soda daily were 18 percent more likely to develop Type 2 diabetes over a sixteen year period compared with those who did not consume soda. Previous studies in the United States found that daily soda consumption increased the risk of Type 2 diabetes by 25 percent. Source: http://www.livescience.com/29024-soda-type-2-diabetes-risk.html

Have you taken the time to look at the food and beverage options you make accessible to your employees at the workplace? Potato chips, chocolate bars, candies, soda pop, cookies, etc. are often the only "food" choices accessible. Really think about this one. A shift to fresh and healthy can happen ... it just requires consciousness and leadership. Employers took cigarette vending machines out the workplace, thankfully, many years ago. I encourage you to be that leader who makes the next progressive step and eliminates the junk food. Look for a supplier with **healthy vending choices**.

Water in a vending machine would seem like a logical and healthy choice however the cost of water (and waste) needs attention. Take for instance, the 20 ounce bottled water generally sold in vending machines alongside soft drinks. Assuming you can find a $2 bottle in a machine, that works out to 10 cents an ounce. Many brand named waters are essentially filtered tap water, bottled close to their distribution point. Most municipal water costs less than 1 cent per gallon.

Now consider another widely sold liquid: gasoline. It has to be pumped out of the ground in the form of crude oil, shipped to a refinery (often halfway across the world), and shipped again to your local filling station. In the U.S. at the time of this book's publication, the average price per gallon is hovering around $2.40.

There are 128 ounces in a gallon, which puts the current price of gasoline at just less than 2 cents an ounce. And that's why there's no shortage of companies that want to get into the business. In terms of price versus production cost, bottled water puts Big Oil to shame.

Bottled water produces up to 1.5 million tons of plastic waste per year. According to Food and Water Watch (http://www.mnn.com/food/healthy-eating/stories/5-reasons-not-to-drink-bottled-water), that plastic requires up to 47 million gallons of oil per year to produce. And while the plastic used to bottle beverages is of high quality and in demand by recyclers, over 80 percent of plastic bottles are simply thrown away.

That assumes empty bottles actually make it to a garbage can. Plastic waste is now at such a volume that vast eddies of current-bound plastic trash now spin endlessly in the world's major oceans. This represents a great risk to marine life, killing birds and fish which mistake our garbage for food. Thanks to its slow decay rate, the vast majority of all plastics ever produced still exist - somewhere.

There's a simple alternative to bottled water: buy a stainless steel thermos, and use it. Don't like the way your local tap water tastes? Inexpensive carbon filters will turn most tap water sparkling fresh at a fraction of bottled water's cost. Do you have **filtered water available at your workplace**? Bottoms up!

Got Deductibles?

Keep your employees happy - get rid of deductibles. I am not a fan of flat dollar one time deductibles. Common amounts are $25 single/$50 family per year or $50 single/$100 family. The reason for this is they don't save a bunch of money and there is the "piss off factor" that will exist with employees. Think about it, an employee that may have one claim in the year for say massage therapy and the treatment cost $75 dollars and plan has a $50 deductible the employee will receive $25 in reimbursement. If they are paying monthly (or not) you can appreciate the dissatisfaction that will be experienced.

You risk the perception of the whole plan being affected by this one ineffective cost containment measure. If you have deductibles have your advisor calculate what it would cost to eliminate them. Your employee satisfaction levels will far exceed the cost to remove the deductibles. Good move, good investment. Go for it.

Wellness: Any company can embrace it. Start small, think big. **Cause a Ruckus!** (See Chapter 12 Wellness).

Visoncare

I don't intend to take away from the value of the full service experience of your local optician. A good article exists online that describes the many considerations when choosing where to shop for optical needs. www.allaboutvision.com/buysmart/eyeglasses.

I will share with you a personal experience in purchasing eyewear recently. Sadly as middle age crept up and caught up to me those road signs and TV onscreen menus became harder to decipher. It was time to accept the fact that squinting made me look old and confused. I was on the back nine of life and I needed glasses.

In many of my presentations I survey the audience informally and ask if anyone had purchased glasses or contacts online. Every year more and more hands go up. When I ask for a description of the experience it is generally described as good to very good. People pull out their eyewear and proudly hold up their glasses and explain that they cost $35 or 3 for $120, etc. Many people described buying multiple pairs to match their wardrobe. Shoes step aside, glasses are apparently the new fashion collectable.

When it came time to take the plunge and get fitted, I visited my local optician who is a great guy and he did a super job of accessing my prescription, lens and frame options. I chose a nice pair of durable Oakely frames with scratch and glare proof lenses. All in, the bill was close to $600 and I was pleased with my experience and the quality of the product.

Due to my curiosity and the growth of online optical we tried an experiment in the office and went online to shop for some additional pairs of glasses.

We tried Zenni Optical www.zennioptical.com and Clearly Contacts www.clearly.ca two well established online retailers with good reputations. We ended up ordering 4 pairs that cost between $30 and $260 each. The cost difference was based on quality and if the frames were a brand name or not. All four pairs arrived in 2-3 weeks, fit nicely and looked good. My kids begged to differ but I hung on to the belief that most teens don't think their dads are very cool and saved my feelings from a demoralizing beat down.

The most common questions I get from employers is "How much does visioncare cost?" or "How much will it cost to increase our visioncare maximum?" The reason I get asked these questions so often is that employees are asking their employers why they don't have visioncare or why the amount is so low. A $200 visioncare benefit every two years is fairly common. I don't generally recommend increasing this maximum as visioncare is not an equitable benefit and online optical now affords the average person the ability to purchase eyewear within the group insurance plan limit. When I say visioncare is not an equitable benefit, the reason is that not every employee uses it. Therefore the more you offer as a benefit, the larger the inequity that exists among employees. This gap is better bridged with as health care spending account (see Chapter 4 "Flex Appeal").

CI - Critical Illness Insurance will pay your employees a tax free amount of money if they are diagnosed with such conditions as heart attack, stroke, cancer and others. Premiums can be employer or employee paid and any amount of coverage can be selected. Premiums can be very affordable. I have lots of CI coverage and I value the protection it offers me and my family.

ASO - If your plan is "fully insured" for health, dental and you haven't considered Administrative Services Only (ASO) i.e. "self-insuring," call your advisor and request this analysis. This one consideration and potential simple change could save your company and employees thousands of dollars a year. If you don't have an ASO contract and you have twenty-five or more employees covered under your benefits plan, you need to look at this option (See Chapter 5 "Pay Me Now or Pay Me Later").

Group RRSP - Make sure you realize that if you are matching employees RRSP contributions you are potentially triggering avoidable payroll taxes such as CPP, EI, Vacation Pay and Worker

Compensation premiums. Ask your advisor to help you avoid these payroll taxes and show you the difference between a Group RRSP, DPSP and DC pension.

Best Doctors - Put it in place for your employees if you don't have it. It will change and quite possibly save lives. (See Chapter 9 "The Best")

For you Simpson's fans:

Mr. Burns while addressing the workers at the power plant:

"Gentlemen! It is imperative that we crush the rebels before the start of the rainy season! And a shiny new donkey for whoever brings me the head of Colonel Montoya."

Smithers hastily whispers something in Burns' ear.

"Oh! And by that I mean it's time to choose the employee of the month!"

Executive benefits can be custom designed to meet the unique needs of managers, owners and executives. The list is long but here are a few to appease the most discerning Mr. Burns' of the corporate world:

Executive medicals, wellness, pension, heath care spending accounts, lifestyle spending accounts, specialty disability coverage, critical Illness insurance, life insurance. Some companies tier their benefits for executives, some don't. There is no right answer and it is more about corporate culture, attraction/retention and philosophy. The above list will give you some ideas to start with if you do decide to tier your plan for your "big shots".

The George Burns Syndrome

You will have employees who live more years in retirement than they spent working. Are you doing anything to help them save for this potential reality? (See Chapter 10 "Got Pension")

CHAPTER 9

THE BEST

I am a big fan of the company ***Best Doctors***.

The value available via the Best Doctors second opinion medical service is incredible. If this company had a theme song it would be "*Best of You*" by the prodigious band Foo Fighters.

"I was too weak to give in

Too strong to lose

My heart is under arrest again

But I break loose

My head is giving me life or death

But I can't choose

I swear I'll never give in

Is someone getting the best, the
best, the best, the best of you?

Has someone taken your faith?

Its real, the pain you feel

You trust, you must

Confess

Is someone getting the best, the
best, the best, the best of you?"

These brilliant lyrics written by Dave Grohl are about breaking away from the things that confine you. They may be interpreted in a variety of ways and to me they suggest that life is too short and precious to not give and get the "best".

We are sometimes confined and do not get the best when it comes to the quality of our health care, for a myriad of reasons ... limited resources, geography, expertise and capacity to name a few.

Best Doctors empowers the average person with the ability to transcend the potential limitations within their medical system. Think of Best Doctors as a world class private medical concierge service for your employees and their families. The concept is simple.

An employee, or their dependent, develops a medical condition, or cannot find a diagnosis for a presenting symptom. Best Doctors provides access to expert medical specialists who help the patient understand their medical condition and treatment options, so they make the right decisions about their care.

The process starts with a call to Best Doctors with a description of the medical challenge and a Best Doctors Member Advocate begins the coordination process. Once all the necessary medical information and reports are gathered, medical specialists perform an in-depth analysis of the medical records, including X-rays, test results, imaging scans and pathology samples. The Best Doctor will review all of the medical records, retest samples if necessary and offer a diagnosis and course of treatment. The expert's detailed summary of findings and recommendations are encouraged to be shared with the local attending physician(s). The intent is a patient-focused model with cooperation and collaboration at the forefront. The impact of this second opinion medical service can be life changing.

I will share with you a very personal story about my experience with Best Doctors. On February 1, 2005 my wife Colleen visited Dr. Susan Robillard, her family physician for a routine check-up. In this appointment Dr. Robillard noticed moles on Colleen's back that seemed unusual in shape and shade. Dr. Robillard referred Colleen to a wonderful local dermatologist named Dr. Mari Wiseman who saw Colleen in her office. Dr. Wiseman examined Colleen and immediately performed an excision removing the moles in question for lab testing. We were curious that the procedure was performed but were not overly concerned. We did not expect the news that we were about to receive.

When the lab reports arrived at Dr. Wiseman's office, she called Colleen for an appointment. Colleen visited Dr. Wiseman and was informed that she was diagnosed with Melanoma and Basel Cell Carcinoma from her separate tissue samples that were tested.

When you receive a cancer diagnosis your world changes - immediately. Panic sets in, you become a frantic overwhelmed amateur internet researcher, and you worry - a lot.

Trying to grasp an understanding of the situation with all the lingo and medical terminology can be perplexing and stressful. Provided below is a sample of the wording from Colleen's lab report:

"Clinical Information: 1) Melanoma Back Re-Excision 2) Suprapubic. Gross: Specimen 1) Consists of an ellipse of the tan skin and subcutaneous fat measuring 4.3, 2.2 cm to a depth of 1.3 cm. Centrally located is an irregularly shaded shiny white lesion with well-defined borders measuring 1.3 x 0.3cm to a height of 0.1 cm. (2 Central cross-sections submitted). Specimen consists of an ellipse of tan skin measuring 1.6 x 0.8 cm to a depth of 0.5 cm. Centrally located is an irregularly shaped pigmented lesion with well-defined borders measuring 1.0 x 0.5 cm with a height of less than 0.1 cm. Resection margins are inked black (2 central cross-section submitted)."

"Diagnosis: 1) Skin (Excision), right lower back - malignant melanoma, superficial spreading type. Clark's level II, Meximial Tumour Thickness 0.5mm. Completely excised with closest lateral margin measuring less than 2mm. 2) Skin (Excision), left thigh - dyplastic nevus, compound type, showing mild cytologic atypia. Completely excised. 3) Skin (biopsy), basal cell carcinoma, superficial type."

From our perspective the report might as well have been written in another language. Dr. Wiseman was awesome and explained the situation in layman's terms to us. She described that Melanoma can be very serious and Basal Cell Carcinoma is not as concerning. She explained that with Melanoma there are two types of staging.

Clinical staging is based on what is found on physical exams, biopsy/removal of the main melanoma, and any imaging tests that are done. Doctors use the pathologic stage if it is available, as it gives a more accurate picture of the extent of the cancer, but in many cases lymph node biopsies are not needed as was the case with Colleen. The T category is based on the thickness of the melanoma and other key factors seen in the skin biopsy.

Tumor thickness: The pathologist looking at the skin biopsy measures the thickness of the melanoma under the microscope.

This is called the Breslow measurement. In general, melanomas less than 1 millimeter (mm) thick (about 1/25 of an inch) have a very small chance of spreading. As the melanoma becomes thicker, it has a greater chance of spreading. Colleen's tumour thickness was measured at .50mm and Dr. Wiseman expressed to us that it was her opinion that the overall risk of the cancer spreading was low.

We had full trust and confidence in Dr. Wiseman's assessment and were very appreciative of her warm demeanor and natural ability of explaining the situation in simple terms which gave us assurance. However, when you are dealing with a cancer diagnosis your mind does not rest.

Prior to Colleen's diagnosis, we fortunately decided to add Best Doctors to our employee benefits program at work. That small decision made an incredible impact on my family and my belief in this valuable second opinion medical service, which I encourage all of my clients to consider adding to their employee benefits package.

The Best Doctors medical panel referred Colleen's case to a renowned Dermatologist who practiced in San Antonio Texas. Upon receipt, all of her medical records and pathology were thoroughly re-reviewed. From the three page "Inter-Consultation" report that was meticulously prepared and provided to us we received a gift. That gift was incredible peace of mind. The Best Doctors report confirmed the findings of Dr. Wiseman that the melanoma was diagnosed early, the cancer had not spread and no further course of treatment was required. Colleen was advised to become a regular patient of Dr. Wiseman and to visit her regularly which she has done, much to Colleen's enjoyment as Dr. Wiseman is delightful. We are blessed that Colleen remains healthy and cancer free to this day and are forever grateful to Dr. Robillard for her diligence and recommendation to consult with our own local world class Dermatologist, Dr. Wiseman.

Best Doctors gave us peace of mind by confirming the excellent medical treatment and consultation we received locally, was supported by the second opinion of one the world's leading skin cancer experts.

A few years later Best Doctors also supported someone very close to us. On August 19, 2011 our dear friend Nancy was diagnosed with Triple Negative Breast Cancer, a very dangerous and more aggressive breast cancer than other types.

Triple Negative Breast Cancer typically does not respond well to hormonal therapy and Herceptin, although it can be treated with chemotherapy and radiation. It is also more likely to recur and metastasize than other subtypes of breast cancer.

Nancy was faced with a decision to have a single mastectomy or a bilateral and felt she had to get a second opinion, which is difficult to obtain and time consuming. Timing was particularly critical in her case.

Having become a Best Doctors member through a private membership, Nancy called them for help. Lauren, a registered nurse, became Nancy's Member Advocate and immediately began the Inter-Consultation for her.

Within three weeks of her call, Nancy received a written report from a Best Doctors specialist in breast cancer. The report recommended a bilateral mastectomy. It went on to explain that without a bilateral mastectomy Nancy had a 24% chance that cancer could reoccur within ten years. She was also told to have genetic testing done, for if she had a gene mutation, she was at a higher risk for ovarian cancer and should therefore have her ovaries and fallopian tubes removed. The Best Doctors specialist gave recommendations for long-term success, with which her oncologist agreed. Nancy had a bilateral mastectomy and testing for the gene mutation and the results today are positive. She is cancer free!

"I am a very positive person, but it was such an emotional and scary time. Lauren kept in touch with me constantly through e-mails while my case was going through Best Doctors process, keeping me informed of what was happening. It was good to receive lots of information from Best Doctors and their recommendation to do a bilateral mastectomy was so great, I've never looked back. They reassured me that I was doing the right thing, especially when I was so pressed for time. It made me feel good about my decisions. Best Doctors is amazing!"

Founded in 1989 by Harvard Medical School physicians, **Best Doctors** serves over 30 million members in 70 countries. Best Doctors has a worldwide network of over 53,000 leading medical specialists in more than 450 specialties and subspecialties that help members ensure they have the right diagnosis and the best treatment. The medical experts in the Best Doctors database are recommended by other doctors through an extensive peer nomination process.

Many **Best Doctors members** receive information and recommendations that literally changes their lives. Statistics from Best Doctors confirm that 60% of member treatments are modified and in 27% of cases there is a change in diagnosis. (Reference: www.bestdoctors.ca) This second opinion medical service has improved the quality of life for members and has saved many lives.

For as little as the cost of one cup of coffee per month your company can add this service to your existing benefits program. The impact Best Doctors has had on my family, loved ones and customers is immeasurable.

CHAPTER 10

GOT PENSION?

This chapter will shed light on the crucial topic of employee planning for retirement. **Got Pension?** is a boiled down summary of what could easily be a complete book dedicated to this vital topic. I found this chapter the hardest to write because of the massive volume of information that needed to be considered and then condensed. I personally believe this topic to be the most important employee benefit consideration that an employer can make, so I sincerely hope I have done my best to keep you focused on the key points that will adequately allow you to consider your organizations best approach to this issue and the options to ponder.

A couple of cute quotes as a warm up:

Retirement is like a long vacation in Vegas. The goal is to enjoy these years to the fullest, but not so fully that you run out of money.

-Jonathan Clements

Retirement at sixty-five is ridiculous. When I was sixty-five I still had pimples.

-George Burns

Unfortunately not everyone will live to one hundred, telling jokes and smoking cigars. George Burn's youthful exuberance is legendary and he brought attention to the concept of longevity well into the golden years. (Chapter 11 Long-Life Secrets will share some more great insights from some admirable Centurions).

For many the question isn't "at what age do you want to retire?" it's "at what income do you want to retire?" (quote by boxing legend George Foreman).

I started in the benefits and pension industry over twenty-five years ago. Employer sponsored retirement programs have always been an extremely important and valuable employee benefit that dramatically influences what income level employees will retire at... and ultimately the lifestyle they experience.

There is a perception that we are not **saving** enough. If we listen to sentiment on why Canadians are not adequately saving for retirement on their own we get a myriad of opinions. I happen to believe that our "supersized" lifestyles have something to do with this. Compare current Canadian society to twenty or thirty years ago. Today houses are bigger, mortgages are larger, credit card debt is more common and there are two or more cars in the driveway. Kids participate in multiple expensive activities, post-secondary education is more of a consideration, everyone has a smartphone and spring vacation often involves a beach. The aforementioned financial commitments often leave family savings for the future limited or non-existent.

So where do retirement savings come from? If we consider the three legged stool a as retirement funding metaphor we can break down each leg as follows: **Government, Employer and Employee.**

1. Government Plans:

If we rely solely on government sponsored retirement programs what does that look like? To keep things simple, government benefits are broken down into Canada Pension Plan (CPP) and Old Age Security. http://www.servicecanada.gc.ca/eng/services/pensions/cpp/payments/index.shtml If you qualify for both at the maximum you can expect to receive about $20,000 per year. If you receive the average you can expect to receive about $15,000 per year. A reasonable amount of money but certainly a modest lifestyle at best if this is an individual's sole or primary source of retirement income. Many retirement planning experts suggest that in retirement the average person will need somewhere between 50-70% of their pre-retirement earnings to maintain their lifestyle in retirement.

Our balanced approach between public and private savings programs has created for Canada one of the top 5 retirement systems in the world according to the OECD. The key to make it work well is that all 3 legs of the stool need to be in play.

2. Employer and Employee Plans

The starting point for all employers as it relates to the topic of retirement is asking the following question:

Do you feel any responsibility towards your employee's financial security in retirement?

If the answer is yes then kudos to your progressive organization. If your company currently has no form of employer sponsored retirement contribution it is with deep respect that I suggest you consider implementing a plan and making a difference. Even a "training wheels" starter plan is a step in the right direction (e.g. 1% employee - 1% employer match). The future financial impact you will have on your people will be meaningful and measurable no matter what formula you choose. On top of that you will have the opportunity of placing your company in the desirable category of "employer of choice".

Employers have an incredible amount of influence and impact related to their employee's future personal financial situation. Based on my experience, I find that *unless an employee participates in an employer sponsored retirement contribution many do not adequately take the initiative to save on their own.*

The most typical employer sponsored retirement plans are in the form of a **matching contribution** via a Group RRSP, DPSP (Deferred Profit Sharing Plan) or Defined Contribution (DC) Pension Plan. For the sake of brevity and simplicity I am going to skip over Defined Benefit (DB), the grand-daddy of pension plans. As an employee member of a DB plan you are likely a government employee or on a legacy plan with a large corporation. If you are on a DB plan consider yourself lucky and rack up your years of service as they are the fuel that drives your future monthly benefit. If you are an employer with a DB plan you are likely considering a windup of the DB plan and converting it to DC plan. Unfunded liabilities, nervous Boards of Directors, longevity risk and expensive administrative costs keep many CEO's, HR VP's and CFO's awake at night.

For the purpose of this chapter the focus will be on the **matching style** of program. That is where the employer puts in a percentage of the employees pay or a flat dollar amount and the employee matches it or vice versa. Some employers don't require an employee match, however that is less likely.

I find that most non-contributory (i.e. no company matching) Group RRSP programs that employers establish for employees to deduct their contributions from payroll on their own don't seem to be well subscribed to. The intention by the employer is admirable but they just don't work on a measurable scale as fund balances and the percentage of employees actually participating is unimpressive. Even the best promoted non-contributory Group RRSP's do not seem to stir up the participation hoped for.

The Defined Contribution Pension Plan

The choice of DC, DPSP or RRSP is dependent on corporate and employee needs and philosophies. There is no right answer, however I am a strong proponent of DC pension for one significant reason - integrity of capital. What I mean by this is when money is accumulated in a DC pension it cannot be unlocked (cashed out) prior to retirement. If you subscribe to the idea that a retirement plan is to guarantee some amount of retirement savings, then you too are a believer in a DC pension plan. In other words the money will be there when it is needed most.

Statistics show that in Canada 75% of DC pensions are mandatory, and only 18% of Group RRSP's are mandatory. So DC pensions have a much better chance of actually providing a retirement income (integrity of capital), as they are likely more often a condition of employment (i.e. mandatory) but also because the funds are locked in for retirement use only. DC pension plans do however come with more complexity and reporting requirements than DPSP's and Group RRSP's. However, a good benefits advisor will be able to sort this out easily for you. Guidance from a benefits advisor will facilitate making the best choice to align with the needs of the organization.

If you answered yes to the question of feeling responsibility towards your employee's financial security in retirement then the next question is:

How much do you contribute?

If you follow the average contribution in Canada it is close to 5%. Specifically, the averages are:

Defined Contribution Pension Plans - Employer 4.9%, Employee 4.3%

Group RRSP Plans - Employer 4.4%, Employee 4.3%

(source: 2015 CAP Benchmark Report)

Many of my trusted and seasoned industry peers promote **the 10% rule**. The belief is that savings should be a minimum of 10% of gross annual income to achieve a comfortable retirement income and lifestyle. My typical client who matches employee contributions, puts in close to the national averages near 5%. However I have clients who match up to 8% which is exceptional, and their generosity is deeply appreciated by the employees who participate.

I recently had a very satisfying conversation with John who worked for years at a client company with a generous match. He was excited to begin his fully funded retirement adventure, which involved buying a motorhome and hitting the open road with his wife, dog and motorcycle in tow.

An often overlooked consideration in retirement income projecting is real estate equity and inheritances. When these considerations are included, the picture does not look so bleak. Models predicting problems in twenty or thirty years are speculative, often relying on questionable assumptions and ignoring home equity, inheritance and behavioral response to personal financial circumstances. The reality is that non-financial assets such as real estate, farm equity, and small business ownership make up the largest percentage of retirement income sources. (source: Statistics Canada; Department of Finance Canada; CPP; QPP; Investor Economics; CIIN; SunLife publication on capital accumulation plans.)

Demographic shifts and rising life expectancy have created a common perception among Canadians that they face a retirement crisis, and that millions will be forced to significantly lower their standard of living when they leave the workforce. Yet the latest research on the subject shows that a strong majority of Canadian households are actually on track to maintain their standard of living in retirement.

This robust retirement readiness does, however, leave 17 percent of the nation's households financially unprepared for retirement. (McKinsey & Company - Building on Canada's Strong Retirement Readiness 2015).

So the sky isn't falling and we shouldn't let the following examples of sensational media headlines discourage or depress us:

"Retirement Slips Further Away For Canadians"

"Large Minority Of Canadians Say They Will Work Till They Die"

"Are Bankrupt Seniors Canada's Future?"

"Retirement Further Out Of Reach: Stats Can"

"There is a widespread retirement readiness crisis in Canada"

"The current framework fails to ensure income replacement in retirement "

The Reality Is:

83% of Canadians are currently on track for retirement.

93% of low-income households are on track due to OAS/GIS and CPP/QPP assets.

77% of mid-to-high income households are on track. (Source: McKinsey & Company: Are Canadians Retirement Ready?)

Those not on track are either not contributing enough to their pension plans, or are without a pension plan and not saving enough on their own. That's where you, the enlightened employer, enters into the equation. A two legged stool is much harder to create balance on than one with three legs!

The Employer Leg

If we look at the employer leg, we find that surprisingly, only approximately 1 in 5 private employers offer any form of employer retirement contribution. The stark reality is that too many Canadians don't participate in an employer sponsored matching retirement program and their retirement savings via a personal RRSP is minimal.

The latest longevity figures from *Statistics Canada* indicate that more Canadians are reaching the 100-year milestone than ever before. We are living longer with an average life expectancy of 84 years. (Source: McKinsey & Company: Are Canadians Retirement Ready?) Those of us who reach age 65 can expect to live on average another twenty years in retirement. That's good news indeed, but it means after having spent roughly forty years in the workforce, pension plan members now face the challenge of providing an income for an additional 50 per cent of that time in retirement. Some people will actually live more years in retirement than they spent working. This can create significant pressures for plan members as the money required to retire comfortably continues to increase. Unfortunately, many are totally unprepared for the significant drop in income that is likely to occur and may struggle financially once they reach retirement age.

At present, approximately only one in four Canadians have an RRSP despite that fact that we are living longer in retirement than ever before. Many Canadians are simply unaware of the potential pending financial shock wave that awaits them in their golden years. Having a strategic approach and a company plan to assist retirement planning helps to create a more sustainable financial future for the ever increasing numbers joining the golden generation. The important thing for members of **employer sponsor retirement plans** is to start planning early, take advantage of their regular income while they work, maximize their tax savings, and build a portfolio that best suits their own retirement needs

As an employer, once you have decided to offer a retirement plan for your employees and have confirmed how much you are going to chip in and the type of plan (DC, DPSP, RRSP), then the rest is relatively easy.

A plan administrator is required and in Canada there are 5 insurance companies who offer the three retirement plan options:

- Desjardins, Great West Life, Industrial Alliance, Manulife and Sun Life.

Some banks offer group retirement programs, however they are generally limited to Group RRSPs. Choosing a supplier is a matter of assessing needs and aligning the best fit. Our firm works with all of the suppliers and sometimes it is a difficult job to differentiate and select **a carrier**, as they all have excellent product and service platforms, being generally competitively priced. A qualified benefits advisor will be able to provide a summary of the carriers available for consideration and help you chose for your best fit.

Once the carrier is chosen, **an investment menu** is selected and offered to the employees. It is most common that the employer leaves the investment choice to the employees and supports their decision with tools and education to select most appropriate based on their investment knowledge, age and tolerance to risk. Target date and target risk funds generally account for 85% of the investment choices selected in today's group retirement programs and these options do an excellent job of aligning investment needs with proper choices and solutions.

A good benefits advisor will help the employer understand the **(CAP) Capital Accumulation Plan Guidelines** which are a formalized set of industry best practices for plan sponsors, plan members, record keepers, investment managers and advisors. The Joint Forum of Financial Market Regulators first released the Guidelines for Capital Accumulation Plans in May 2004. The CAP guidelines help to eliminate grey areas often associated with plan sponsors' responsibilities and governance requirements. The CAP guidelines establish defined practices, good communication (See Chapter 7 "Benefits Communication") and clearly specify sponsor accountability. Following them closely and subscribing to regular documentation will set you and your employees up for success!

It is important to have a good plan and a good advisor to help you deliver on your company's vision of your employee's retirement. With both, "getting pension" is much easier than it may seem.

CHAPTER 11

LONG-LIFE SECRETS

I was filling up with gas recently at my neighborhood station and noticed a special Time Magazine edition with the bold title "Secrets of Living Longer". As I am a student of wellness with a curiosity in longevity (I hope to see age 100) I ended up buying it.

The magazine was fascinating with many great stories. One section was completely devoted to cute quotes from elders who have defied the odds and lived to age 99 or beyond. Below are some of the best, with the first one being my favourite:

"My secret to a long life has been staying away from men. They're just more trouble than they're worth. I also made sure that I got plenty of exercise, eat a nice warm bowl of porridge every morning, and never gotten married."

-Jessie Callahan, Oldest woman in Scotland at age 107

"Mind your own business and don't eat junk food."

- Besse Cooper at age 116

"Have a good wife, two scotches a night, and be easygoing"

- Samuel Ball at age 102

"Raising my kids helped me live this long. My family has always given me meaning. Having friends helps too"

- Justina Sotomayor at age 100

"Kindness. Treat people right and be nice to other people."

Gertrude Weaver, a Supercententenarian from Arkansas at age 116

"I live on green vegetables and fruit. I bathe my feet every night and massage them in olive oil."

- Bernando LaPallo at age 111

"I wonder about that too"

- Misao Okawa at age 117, on how she lived so long

"I participate in lots of activities. I play bingo, do meditation and crafts, and attend fitness classes, like Zumba, Chair Yoga and Sittercise"

- Mae Lewis at age 100

"I do a lot of good deeds, so maybe that's helped"

- Rose Strassburger at age 100

"I don't eat very much. But I always eat a fruit, a vegetable, and a little meat"

- Louis Charpentier at age 99

"I used to own a restaurant and worked 14 hours a day, six days a week....These days I just try and stay *independent."*

- Haru Ito at age 100

"I've never been to a beauty shop. I've never been vain."

- Adelina Domingues at age 114

"Friends, a good cigar, drinking lots of good water, no alcohol, staying positive and lots of singing will keep you alive for a long time."

- Christian Mortensen at age 115

"If you're positive you can get through (life) Ok. When you think negatively, you're putting poison on your body. Just smile. They say laughter is the best medicine there is."

- Elsa Bailey at age 100

"Love people. Find something to like about the person - it's there - because we're all just people."

- Lucille Boston Lewis at age 100

"I left school when I was 12, but I traveled the world, and that was my education. People interested me then and still do...I remain very curious about life, and if something new happens, I want to be involved."

- Lili Rudin at age 100

"There is no need to ever retire, but if one must, it should be a lot later than 65."

- Shigeaki Hinohara at age 100

Brilliant all of them!

CHAPTER 12

WELLNESS

"I have no special talents. I am only passionately curious" ~ Albert Einstein

This quote sums up my personal and professional feelings towards wellness. I don't profess to be an expert in this field but it is a topic that I am deeply passionate about. I believe that corporate sponsored wellness is the next substantial employee benefits movement and a proactive attraction and retention strategy initiated by employers. My company has committed to doing a "deep dive" into this space with the goal of helping employers sort out and implement a meaningful corporate sponsored wellness program. The journey excites me.

If there is a section from this book I would like you to really put some thought into it is this one. I am going to challenge you with this one simple question:

As an employer do you feel any responsibility towards your employee's personal wellness?

If you are not sure what I mean by this, allow me to reframe the question:

Do you care about your employee's personal wellbeing with respect to their body, mind and spirit and if so, are you prepared to do anything about it?

If the answer is no, it is with deep respect that I compel you to put some serious thought to your position and open your mind to the organizational possibilities. If the answer is yes, my esteemed enlightened reader who possesses incredible awesomeness ... **you are the light!**

My wellness mentor is Dr. James Rouse (www.drjamesrouse.com). He is the most positive, fit and holistic person I have ever known. Dr. James is a world class wellness guru and author from Colorado with over thirty years of experience in his field. It is his life's mission to promote self-care and self-love. He regularly consults to best-in-class companies such as Google and Cisco and has shared the stage with world renowned speakers such as Dr. Mehmet Oz, Seth Godin and Sir Richard Branson. Dr. James is a naturopathic doctor, entrepreneur, certified yoga instructor, magazine founder, radio talk show host, QVC Network Wellness Doctor, Ironman triathlete.

He does it all and I have had the very good fortune to have my friend Dr. James spend time and share his deep wisdom with "my tribe": family, friends and clients. Dr. James sums it up by describing corporate sponsored wellness as, **"assisting employees to make good on good intentions".**

A recent powerful session that Dr. James facilitated for our tribe was incredibly transformational as we learned how to "live a day in the life of epic well-being," focusing on the mind, body, spirit. I may have just opened myself up to being accused by some of waxing poetic on "rainbows and unicorns" but it was a very personal, meaningful and connective experience. All in attendance were moved and continue to work on their practice. A useful summary from the session on how you can influence organizational wellness is as follows:

- Be a role model/lead by example - let your actions speak louder than your words
- Perform random acts of kindness
- Create happiness by hugging for 3 - 7 secs
- Give positive recognition daily
- Educate instead of mandating or preaching
- Ask coworkers - What's the *why* that motivates them?
- Place props or visual cues up around the office
- Lean on existing networks and peers for support
- Weave wellness into the very fabric of your corporate culture
- Create a wellness committee or health coordinator role

- ❖ Present wellness as a business case to executives

I will share with you a story. I debated including it in this chapter because it is personal.

Inspired by Dr. James and other life mentors, I recently made the commitment to get into the best physical and mental shape of my life. Not easy in your late 40's trust me! I can tell you after making this commitment in the last year, I am proud to have reached my goal ... and the impact on my feeling of well-being and overall energy has been dramatic. I have lost twenty pounds from my high water mark, get up at 5:00 am on most days, drink more water, treasure my important relationships, exercise five times per week, mediate and have more jam than I have ever known. I eat smarter, drink way less beer and have learned to savour wine instead of guzzling it. Don't get me wrong, I still like to have a good time, drink more Prosecco than ever and love a fun party. I am pissed at myself for not committing earlier in life to a healthier more holistic lifestyle, but I am happy to be late to the party.

I have decided to not be shy about sharing my personal goals with family, friends and colleagues, as I find the more people I share my personal wellness aspirations with, the more committed to my goals and lifestyle I become. This has been a change for me, as I have traditionally held my personal and professional aspirations close. I may not make it to my long goal of reaching age 100, but I am going to die trying! I believe the passion to pursue personal wellness is contagious and your herd can become a cohesive motivated tribe if you make the commitment.

Wellness is a broad and massive topic, lives at the personal level and it means different things to different people. My company has embraced wellness whole heartedly and offers access to a variety of programs to our team that are designed to assist them make good lifestyle choices with respect to nutrition, education, health, fitness and family, on a free or subsidized basis. Corporate sponsored wellness is not a one-size-fits-all approach, but rather a customized suit that is dependent upon size, culture, geographic location and budget. However, any sized company can jump in and take the plunge.

My intent is not to suggest silver bullet turn-key wellness solutions, but rather to expose examples of the various corporate sponsored programs that I have seen that are successful. By successful, I mean the employers have invested and implemented and the employees have bought in, making personal gains in their overall personal wellness.

The ultimate goal is to influence healthy choices, improve employees' overall health and provide a ROI to both the company and the employees.

The ultimate win - win.

It is not a stretch to believe that the person who moves around more, eats better, gets proper sleep and engages in healthy and meaningful personal relationships, will generally be healthier and happier. Simple cause and effect ... if your employees are healthier and happier they will be mentally present and more productive. If your CEO or CFO needs proof of ROI there are many well documented studies that illustrate up to a $6 return to every $1 invested. Data supports that wellness programs save about 1.5 to 1.7 days in absenteeism per worker over 12 months or an estimated $251 per employee per year in savings. (Reference - Sun Life Ivey ROI Study, phase 1).

The foundation of an effective corporate sponsored wellness program is *belief*. So if you are a believer, how can you get involved and make a difference in your employee's personal wellness and your corporate culture? I assert that it starts with leadership at the ownership and/or senior management level. Successful corporate sponsored wellness is not something that can be delegated then not embraced at all levels. It is also not about weight loss contests or promoting trendy diets. It is the endorsing of an overall holistic approach that involves the mind, body and spirit of your people.

Six years after launching its wellness program, London Hydro couldn't be happier with the results — and momentum continues to build.

"Since 2009, we've seen a 30% reduction in sick leave," says Jeff Harrison, manager of health and safety for the London, Ontario-based company of 330 employees. Equally important are the results that are more difficult to quantify.

"You can see employees feel better about themselves, and this benefits our culture. It creates a family feeling at work."

When asked what advice he would give to other employers, Harrison boiled the wellness equation down to three components:

1. Bring in the experts

From the get-go, London Hydro hired an independent wellness firm, which works with management and a volunteer committee of employees.

"We could not be at this level without them," says Harrison.

The provider organizes events, employs health coaches and supplies detailed reports to management.

2. Make it personal

In 2014, 97% of the company's office employees regularly participated in the monthly, one-on-one health coaching sessions. The coaches develop individual wellness goals based on health risk screenings, and aggregate results so far include reductions in cancer risk from 71% in 2009 to45% in 2014, and in high stress levels from 34% to 19%. Group programs and events help employees reach personal goals. For employees working in the field, the health coaches give presentations at health and safety meetings and regularly reach out with more of a personal touch — for example, serving fresh porridge with berries prior to the start of the work day.

3. Take internal stock

London Hydro also assessed its work environment.

“We are always looking for ways to improve our culture,” says Harrison.

Changes over the last year include the renovation of the cafeteria into an internet café, with Chromebook computers, televisions and, of course, a range of healthy foods, a quiet room where employees can relax and an updated fitness centre that’s open 24/7. (Reference: Sanofi Canada Healthcare Survey | 2015.)

Wellness has been defined in many ways, but a general understanding is that wellness (sometimes called well-being) is broader than health and usually includes a state of balance in body, mind (emotional and intellectual), spirit and social domains, with an emphasis on prevention and resilience.

It incorporates the quality of a person's life as well as general life satisfaction. It often means having a sense of purpose and mastery over life. Importantly, wellness is not the same for everyone: it includes subjective, perceptual and relative elements. Wellness is seen as a continuum measured in degrees, rather than a discrete condition. (Reference: 10. British Columbia Atlas of Wellness, First (2007) and Second (2011) editions. Sanofi Canada Healthcare Survey 2015)

In the workplace, that description probably seems unattainable and may appear disconnected from an employer's goals and interests. So, wellness is often reduced to a series of fitness and health education programs that are typically sporadic, not evaluated for need or impact, and not integrated with one another or with the organization's strategy. Sometimes wellness programs simply focus on the individual's lifestyle, such as exercise, diet, weight, smoking, alcohol, stress, and overlook the employer's ability to influence health through leadership and management policies, programs, and practices. These latter factors create a culture that employees interpret in order to gauge levels of trust, fairness, respect, recognition and support. Lifestyle is certainly important but it is not sufficient to determine health and it does not exist in a vacuum. Beyond work, wellness is influenced at home, in the community and by the broader environment.

Based on many years of experience in this field, the following definition of a healthy organization is the best I've come across:

". . . one whose culture, climate, and practices create an environment that promotes both employee health and safety as well as organizational effectiveness." (Reference Lim S-Y, LR Murphy. The Relationship of Organizational Factors to Employee Health and Overall Effectiveness. American Journal of Industrial Medicine 1999:36(Suppl):64–65.)

This is short, simple, integrative and adaptable. Beyond a program or a slogan or the best of intentions, this should become our **benchmark for wellness at work**.

Inherently then, wellness should be strategic and therefore sustained. It ought to focus on education and behaviour at all levels of the organization, and aim to improve the worker, the workplace and the employer. (Reference - Chris Bonnett, H3 Consulting, Sanofi Canada Healthcare Survery 2015)

Culturally Wellness can be a part of your corporate culture and organizational belief system. Think about this way, your employees will spend on average over 2000 hours a year committed to you. Some will spend more time with their work associates than their family. Some employees will spend time away from their families for you, work excessive hours and even put themselves at some risk. Yes they are compensated for their time but is this where the obligation ends? Do you as the employer feel morally responsible to help your employees make good lifestyle choices? I suppose it comes down to what degree of paternalism is embraced corporately. I have confidence in the belief that corporate sponsored wellness is smart because it is morally admirable but also strategic and I believe will deliver pardon the pun, a "healthy" return on investment if done properly.

Starting small is ok because personal wellness beliefs are not formed immediately and habits do not change overnight. Bringing in speakers over the lunch hour to talk about the importance of getting enough sleep, eating better or engagement in meaningful communication with family and loved ones is a good start. Simple changes such as adding healthy choices to the lunch room or vending machines are also great initiatives. I have seen employers provide free fruits and vegetables and/or subsidize the cost of fresh cold pressed vegetable and fruit juice. Comprehensive health risk self-assessments, free health checks with registered nurses, online health risk assessments and wellness sessions on a variety of topics such as those previously mentioned, can be offered to employees. One of my progressive clients allows pets at work and extends to me the joy of bringing Duke my chocolate lab to my meetings with them.

Technology has allowed us to leverage our computers, smartphones and the internet in the pursuit of sponsoring and implementing wellness at work. There are some really cool companies out there who offer amazing tech assisted apps and wellness options. Fit Bit, Nike, Virgin Pulse, Sprout, MediResource and Ceridian, are just a few to consider from many. A quick Google search can provide a multitude of great resources and options to consider.

You shouldn't obsess with perfect execution because it's not about nailing your wellness program right at the start. More importantly it is about pushing away from the inertia, starting change and influencing good choices and behaviours. Your employees will love you for it!

Here is a tip. The implementation of an **Employee Assistance Program** is a good start towards sponsoring wellness at work. Per month, for as little as the cost of one fancy coffee drink, you can provide your employees access to private and confidential counselling, concierge services and information that will help them deal with a myriad of distracting and consuming issues that we are all faced with at some time in our lives. Here is some simple advice, if you don't have an EAP, considering getting one and if you do invest in an EAP program, make your employees well aware of it. You will make a difference in their lives when they need it most. The benefit to you is that your employees will appreciate it and they will be more present at work, which is a nice by-product of your investment in them.

So in summary, please consider doing something. Speak to your benefits advisor, book "lunch and learns", put wellness on your next management meeting agenda, engage your CEO in conversation around the topic, start a discussion, start a committee, create a micro revolution that will lead to macro changes in your employees and corporate culture.

It starts with you. Be brave. Have fun doing it! You won't regret it and it may well be the best thing you ever do for your organization.

CLOSING THOUGHTS

I wrote this book because I could not find it in the marketplace. I believed that employers needed a simple, approachable and easy-to-read handbook (not textbook) to navigate the complicated waters of employee benefits.

Filling the existing editorial void by conceiving, handcrafting and publishing this book has been one of the most challenging but beautiful professional experiences I have ever had. Giving back to an industry that has given me so much has been such a privilege.

I am proud to have shared with you the knowledge of my life's work that will hopefully provoke thought, encourage discovery, inspire discussion and ultimately drive positive change. I sincerely thank you for taking the time to read my first book and I am humbled by your interest in it.

I would love to hear from you should you wish to chime in on your *Bubble Wrap* reading experience.

With deep gratitude,

Kevin McFadden

kevin@mcfaddenbenefits.com